conte

2
cooking in the microwave

4—59
recipes

32—33
vegetables in the microwave

60—61
glossary

62
index

63
facts and figures

British & North American Readers:
Please note that Australian cup and spoon measurements are metric. A quick conversion guide appears on page 63. A glossary explaining unfamiliar terms and ingredients begins on page 60.

2 cooking in the microwave

As a general rule, if food needs to be turned, covered or stirred when cooked conventionally, it is also necessary to do the same in the microwave oven. If you're unsure about cooking times, go for a shorter period – you can always return the food to your microwave oven to cook it longer, but initial overcooking will ruin your food.

Standing time
This is an important aspect of microwave cooking and shouldn't be ignored. Food continues to cook for a few minutes after it has been removed from the oven. Standing time varies according to the size and density of the food. If standing time isn't taken into consideration, your dish could overcook. Keep food covered during standing time.

Cookware
There's a great range of cookware designed for use in the microwave oven. But you'll find you can use most of the dishes you have in your kitchen. China, glass and some earthenware are all suitable. Metal is not. Dishes with a gold or silver rim are unsuitable. To be absolutely sure that a dish is microwave-safe, stand it in the oven with a glass of water next to it. Cook on HIGH for 1 minute. If the dish remains cold, it is fine to use. If it gets hot (like the water), don't use the dish in your microwave oven.

Covering food
- The dish containing the food may be covered with plastic wrap, a plate or a lid.

- Bacon cooks well when placed in a single layer on 2 sheets of absorbent paper, and covered loosely with 2 more sheets of absorbent paper. The paper absorbs the fat and prevents spattering.
- When you buy takeaway food in a covered plastic container, either transfer it to a microwave-safe dish before reheating, or, if you're microwaving for a very short time, remove the lid and cover the container with plastic wrap. The thin plastic used by most takeaway food outlets will not tolerate microwave energy for very long – it can become soft and, with prolonged cooking, it will sometimes even melt – right into tonight's dinner.

Shielding

Use small pieces of foil to cover the corners of square or rectangular containers to prevent overcooking. Foil should also be wrapped around chicken wing tips and the bony end of drumsticks when cooking a whole bird.

Cautionary notes

- Metal twist ties and metal skewers are not suitable for use in the microwave oven.
- Long cooking in the microwave oven will heat china and glass dishes; make sure you remove them with oven mitts.
- When removing plastic wrap from a microwaved dish, peel it from the back of the dish to protect your hands and face from the steam.
- Bones and fat conduct heat so the meat next to them will cook more quickly than the rest of the meat. This is one reason why standing time for meat dishes is so essential. 
- When cooking food having one end thicker than another, for example, a chicken drumstick, place the thinner end towards the centre of the dish and the thicker end on the outside. The food will cook more evenly when arranged in this particular way.

spicy   5
indian-style fish

We used blue-eye for this recipe.

750g thick boneless white fish fillets

2 tablespoons ghee

1 large (200g) onion, sliced

4 cloves garlic, crushed

1 tablespoon grated fresh ginger

3 teaspoons ground coriander

3 teaspoons ground cumin

1/2 teaspoon cayenne pepper

2 x 400g cans tomatoes

1/2 cup (125ml) cream

1 tablespoon lemon juice

2 tablespoons chopped fresh coriander leaves

Cut fish into 4cm pieces.
Meanwhile combine ghee and onion in large shallow microwave-safe dish; cook, uncovered, on HIGH (100%) about 8 minutes or until onion is browned lightly, stirring 3 times during cooking. Add garlic, ginger and spices; cook, uncovered, on HIGH (100%) 30 seconds. Add undrained crushed tomatoes, cream and juice; cook, uncovered, on HIGH (100%) 7 minutes, stirring once during cooking.
Add fish, in single layer; cook, uncovered, on HIGH (100%) about 8 minutes or until fish is tender. Just before serving, sprinkle with fresh coriander leaves.

On the table in 30 minutes

6 asparagus and chicken
risotto

300g asparagus, chopped

2 tablespoons olive oil

1½ cups (300g) arborio rice

1 clove garlic, crushed

4 cups (1 litre) boiling chicken stock

2 cups (340g) coarsely chopped cooked chicken

¼ cup (20g) coarsely grated parmesan cheese

¼ cup (60ml) cream

Place asparagus in large microwave-safe bowl; cook, covered, on HIGH (100%) 1 minute. Rinse asparagus under cold water; drain.

Combine oil, rice and garlic in large microwave-safe bowl; cook, covered, on HIGH (100%) 1 minute. Add 2 cups (500ml) boiling stock; cook, covered, on HIGH (100%) 5 minutes. Add remaining boiling stock; cook, covered, on HIGH (100%) 5 minutes, stirring twice during cooking.

Gently stir asparagus and remaining ingredients into risotto; cook, covered, on HIGH (100%) 2 minutes. Stand, covered, 5 minutes.

On the table in 25 minutes

country-style beef
rissoles

500g minced beef

1 small (80g) onion, grated

1 clove garlic, crushed

1 tablespoon barbecue sauce

1 tablespoon tomato sauce

1 tablespoon Worcestershire sauce

1 cup (70g) stale breadcrumbs

1 egg, beaten lightly

1 teaspoon chopped fresh thyme

2 tablespoons chopped fresh parsley

1 small (130g) tomato, chopped

glaze

1/4 cup (60ml) barbecue sauce

2 teaspoons Worcestershire sauce

On the table in 25 minutes

Using hand, combine all ingredients in large bowl; shape into 8 patties, about 7cm wide. Place patties around edge of large oiled shallow microwave-safe dish.

Brush patties with Glaze; cook, uncovered, on HIGH (100%) about 7 minutes or until cooked through. Serve sprinkled with extra chopped parsley, if desired.

Glaze Combine sauces in small bowl.

8 curried vegetable soup

Combine oil and onion in large microwave-safe bowl; cook, uncovered, on HIGH (100%) about 8 minutes or until onion is browned lightly, stirring 3 times during cooking. Add ground spices, curry leaves, carrot, potato, mushrooms, stock and puree; cook, uncovered, on HIGH (100%) 15 minutes, stirring once during cooking. Add juice and milk; cook, uncovered, on HIGH (100%) about 10 minutes or until vegetables are tender, stirring twice during cooking. Add peas; cook, uncovered, on HIGH (100%) 2 minutes. Just before serving, stir in fresh coriander leaves.

On the table in 40 minutes

2 teaspoons vegetable oil

1 large (200g) onion, chopped

2 teaspoons ground coriander

1 teaspoon garam masala

1/2 teaspoon chilli powder

6 curry leaves

2 large (360g) carrots, chopped

2 large (600g) potatoes, chopped

100g button mushrooms, chopped

3 cups (750ml) vegetable stock

425g can tomato puree

2 tablespoons lemon juice

1/2 cup (125ml) coconut milk

1/2 cup (60g) frozen peas

2 tablespoons chopped fresh coriander leaves

creamy mushroom
fish

9

40g butter

1 medium (150g) onion, chopped

2 teaspoons chopped fresh thyme

250g button mushrooms, sliced

4 (800g) boneless white fish fillets

2 tablespoons dry white wine

1/4 cup (60ml) fish stock

3 teaspoons cornflour

1/3 cup (80ml) cream

Combine butter, onion and thyme in large shallow microwave-safe dish; cook, uncovered, on HIGH (100%) 4 minutes, stirring once during cooking. Place mushrooms in same dish; top with fish, folding thin ends under. Pour over wine and stock; cook, covered, on HIGH (100%) about 5 minutes or until fish is just cooked through. Remove fish from dish; cover to keep warm. **Reserve** 1 cup (250ml) liquid in dish, stir in blended cornflour and cream; cook, uncovered, on HIGH (100%) about 4 minutes or until sauce boils and thickens slightly, stirring once during cooking. Serve sauce over fish.

On the table in 30 minutes

10 saucy chicken in
yogurt

750g chicken tenderloins

2 cups (500ml) bottled satay sauce

2 large (400g) onions, cut into wedges

250g cherry tomatoes, halved

1/3 cup shredded fresh basil leaves

200ml yogurt

2 tablespoons sweet chilli sauce

Combine chicken, half the satay sauce and onion in large microwave-safe bowl; cook, uncovered, on HIGH (100%) 10 minutes, stirring twice during cooking. Add remaining satay sauce; cook, covered, on HIGH (100%) about 2 minutes or until chicken is cooked through.
Add tomatoes and basil; cook, uncovered, on HIGH (100%) 2 minutes. Serve drizzled with combined yogurt and chilli sauce.

On the table in 30 minutes

corned beef 11

with parsley sauce

1.5kg piece beef corned silverside

2 cups (500ml) water

2 tablespoons brown malt vinegar

2 tablespoons brown sugar

1 medium (150g) onion, quartered

parsley sauce

30g butter

1 small (80g) onion, chopped finely

1 tablespoon plain flour

1 cup (250ml) milk

1 tablespoon chopped fresh parsley

Rinse beef under cold water to remove excess salt.
Place beef in large microwave-safe oven bag with water, vinegar, sugar and onion; secure bag loosely with a rubber band. Place bag in large shallow microwave-safe dish; cook on HIGH (100%) 10 minutes; carefully turn beef upside down. Cook on MEDIUM (55%) 50 minutes; rotating beef twice during cooking. Stand beef 10 minutes in bag while preparing the Parsley Sauce.
Parsley Sauce
Combine butter and onion in medium microwave-safe bowl; cook, uncovered, on HIGH (100%) 2 minutes. Add flour; cook, uncovered, on HIGH (100%) 30 seconds. Whisk in milk and parsley; cook, uncovered, on HIGH (100%) about 3 minutes or until sauce boils and thickens, whisking once during cooking.
On the table in 1¼ hours

12 vegetable chowder

20g butter

1 medium (150g) onion, chopped

2 cloves garlic, crushed

3 bacon rashers, chopped

1½ cups (375ml) vegetable stock

1 stick celery, chopped

1 medium (120g) carrot, chopped

1 medium (200g) potato, chopped

½ medium (200g) kumara, chopped

2 x 130g cans corn kernels, drained

2 tablespoons plain flour

1¾ cups (430ml) milk

2 tablespoons chopped fresh thyme

1 tablespoon Dijon mustard

¼ cup (60ml) cream

½ cup (40g) finely grated parmesan cheese

Combine butter, onion, garlic and bacon in large microwave-safe bowl; cook, uncovered, on HIGH (100%) 5 minutes, stirring once during cooking. Reserve ¼ cup (60ml) stock, add remaining stock to bowl with celery, carrot, potato, kumara and corn; cook, covered, on HIGH (100%) 12 minutes, stirring once during cooking. Add blended flour and reserved stock, milk, thyme and mustard; cook, uncovered, on HIGH (100%) about 5 minutes or until soup boils and thickens slightly, stirring once during cooking. Stir in cream; serve sprinkled with parmesan cheese.

On the table in 40 minutes

hearty bean
soup

1 tablespoon olive oil

1 medium (150g) onion, chopped

1 clove garlic, crushed

300g can butter beans, rinsed, drained

300g can red kidney beans, rinsed, drained

400g can tomatoes

2 tablespoons tomato paste

2 cups (500ml) hot water

1 teaspoon chopped fresh oregano

60g piece spicy salami, chopped

2 tablespoons shredded fresh basil leaves

Combine oil, onion and garlic in large microwave-safe bowl; cook, uncovered, on HIGH (100%) 4 minutes, stirring once during cooking. Add beans, undrained crushed tomatoes, paste, hot water and oregano; cook, covered, on HIGH (100%) 10 minutes.
Stir in salami; serve sprinkled with basil.

On the table in 20 minutes

14 chicken in coconut peanut sauce

1 tablespoon peanut oil

1 medium (150g) onion, chopped

2 cloves garlic, crushed

1 teaspoon grated fresh ginger

4 (680g) chicken breast fillets, sliced thinly

2 teaspoons grated lemon rind

1 teaspoon mild curry powder

1/2 teaspoon ground cumin

3 medium (360g) zucchini

1 cup (250ml) coconut milk

1/3 cup (85g) smooth peanut butter

1/3 cup (80ml) chicken stock

1 teaspoon soy sauce

Combine oil, onion, garlic and ginger in large shallow microwave-safe dish; cook, uncovered, on HIGH (100%) 4 minutes, stirring once during cooking. Add chicken, rind, curry powder and cumin; cook, covered, on HIGH (100%) 5 minutes, stirring once during cooking.

Cut zucchini into thin slices lengthways. Add zucchini and remaining ingredients to chicken mixture in dish; cook, uncovered, on HIGH (100%) about 5 minutes or until zucchini is tender, stirring twice during cooking. Serve sprinkled with paprika, for extra colour, if desired.

On the table in 25 minutes

barbecued pork
stir-fry

15

10 Chinese dried mushrooms
1 tablespoon peanut oil
1 teaspoon sesame oil
2 cloves garlic, crushed
4 green onions, chopped
375g Chinese barbecued pork, sliced thinly
500g fresh thin egg noodles
3 teaspoons cornflour
1 cup (250ml) chicken stock
2 tablespoons soy sauce
1/2 teaspoon ground cumin
1/2 teaspoon ground coriander
250g snow peas, halved
4 cups (320g) shredded Chinese cabbage
1 cup (80g) bean sprouts

Place mushrooms in small heatproof bowl, cover with boiling water, stand 20 minutes. Drain mushrooms, discard stems, slice caps thinly.
Combine peanut oil, sesame oil, garlic and onion in large microwave-safe bowl; cook, uncovered, on HIGH (100%) 1 minute. Add mushrooms, pork and noodles. Stir in blended cornflour and stock, sauce and spices; cook, uncovered, on HIGH (100%) 6 minutes, stirring once during cooking. Add snow peas, cabbage and sprouts; cook, uncovered, on HIGH (100%) about 3 minutes or until mixture boils and thickens slightly.

On the table in 30 minutes

16 middle eastern-style meatballs

1 tablespoon olive oil

1 large (200g) onion, chopped

2 cloves garlic, crushed

2 teaspoons ground ginger

1 teaspoon ground coriander

2 teaspoons ground cumin

1/4 teaspoon ground cinnamon

1/3 cup (50g) dried currants

2 tablespoons chopped fresh coriander leaves

1/3 cup (55g) blanched almonds, chopped

1kg minced beef

1 tablespoon sambal oelek

1 cup (70g) stale breadcrumbs

1 egg, beaten lightly

yogurt sauce

1 1/2 cups (375ml) yogurt

2 (260g) Lebanese cucumbers, seeded, chopped

1/4 cup chopped fresh mint leaves

2 teaspoons lemon juice

17

Combine oil, onion, garlic and ground spices in large microwave-safe bowl; cook, uncovered, on HIGH (100%) 5 minutes, stirring once during cooking. Add currants, fresh coriander, nuts, beef, sambal oelek, breadcrumbs and egg; mix well. Shape quarter cups of mixture into balls.
Place meatballs, in single layer, in large oiled shallow microwave-safe dish. Cook, uncovered, in 2 batches, on HIGH (100%) about 7 minutes or until cooked through. Serve hot or cold meatballs with Yogurt Sauce.
Yogurt Sauce Place all ingredients in small bowl. Mix well.

On the table in 40 minutes

18 pumpkin and leek soup

40g butter

1 large (500g) leek, sliced

1kg butternut pumpkin, chopped

2 medium (400g) potatoes, chopped

4 cups (1 litre) chicken stock

1/2 cup (125ml) milk

1/2 cup (125ml) cream

Combine butter and leek in large microwave-safe bowl; cook, covered, on HIGH (100%) 5 minutes, stirring once during cooking. Add pumpkin, potato and 1/2 cup (125ml) of the stock; cook, covered, on HIGH (100%) about 20 minutes or until pumpkin and potato are tender, stirring twice during cooking. Stir in remaining stock and milk.

Blend or process pumpkin mixture, in batches, until smooth. Return mixture to large microwave-safe bowl; cook, covered, on HIGH (100%) about 5 minutes or until heated through, stirring once during cooking. Ladle soup into serving bowls; swirl cream into soup.

On the table in 40 minutes

microwave chicken 19
and potato slice

You will need 1 cooked chicken for this recipe.

750g potatoes, sliced thickly

20g butter

2½ cups (425g) cooked chopped chicken

6 green onions, chopped

1 small (150g) red capsicum, chopped

30g butter, extra

1 clove garlic, crushed

2 tablespoons plain flour

⅓ cup (80ml) chicken stock

⅓ cup (80ml) dry white wine

½ cup (125ml) cream

2 teaspoons French mustard

1 tablespoon mayonnaise

½ cup (60g) coarsely grated cheddar cheese

pinch sweet paprika

2 tablespoons chopped fresh parsley

Layer potatoes in 2.5-litre (10-cup) shallow microwave-safe dish, top with butter; cook, covered, on HIGH (100%) 10 minutes. Top with chicken, onion and capsicum.

Place extra butter and garlic in medium microwave-safe bowl; cook, uncovered, on HIGH (100%) 30 seconds. Stir in flour, water, crumbled stock cube, wine and cream; cook, uncovered, on HIGH (100%) about 3 minutes or until sauce boils and thickens, whisking once during cooking. Whisk in combined mustard and mayonnaise.

Pour sauce over chicken in dish, sprinkle with cheese and paprika. Cook, uncovered, on HIGH (100%) 5 minutes. Serve sprinkled with parsley.

On the table in 45 minutes

20 sesame mustard
chicken

¾ cup (110g) sesame seeds

½ cup (125ml) sour cream

2 tablespoons seeded mustard

1 teaspoon grated orange rind

4 (680g) chicken breast fillets

Place sesame seeds in large shallow microwave-safe dish; cook, uncovered, on HIGH (100%) about 7 minutes or until browned lightly, stirring 3 times during cooking.

Combine sour cream, mustard, rind and chicken in large bowl; mix well. Toss chicken in seeds, place in single layer, in large shallow microwave-safe dish; cook, covered, on HIGH (100%) about 8 minutes or until cooked through.

On the table in 20 minutes

spicy peppered steak

21

750g beef fillet steak, sliced thinly

1 tablespoon coarsely ground black pepper

1 small (150g) red capsicum, sliced

1 small (150g) green capsicum, chopped finely

6 green onions, chopped

1½ tablespoons cornflour

½ cup (125ml) water

3 teaspoons grated fresh ginger

3 cloves garlic, crushed

2 tablespoons soy sauce

1 teaspoon sesame oil

On the table in 30 minutes

Combine all ingredients in large microwave-safe bowl; mix well. Cook, covered, on HIGH (100%) 10 minutes, stirring once during cooking.
Uncover; cook on MEDIUM (55%) 10 minutes, stirring twice during cooking.

22 mexican chilli beef

1 tablespoon olive oil

1 medium (150g) onion, chopped

2 cloves garlic, crushed

1kg minced beef

1 medium jalapeno pepper, chopped finely

400g can tomatoes

1 cup (250ml) beef stock

¾ cup (180ml) tomato paste

425g can Mexican-style baked beans

2 tablespoons chopped fresh parsley

Combine oil, onion and garlic in large microwave-safe bowl; cook, uncovered, on HIGH (100%) 4 minutes, stirring once during cooking. **Stir** in beef; cook, uncovered, on HIGH (100%) 10 minutes, stirring twice. Add jalapeno, undrained crushed tomatoes, stock and paste. **Cook**, uncovered, on HIGH (100%) about 25 minutes or until thick, stirring twice. Stir in beans; cook, uncovered, on HIGH (100%) 2 minutes. Stir in pàrsley.

On the table in 45 minutes

vegetable
and nut curry

1 tablespoon peanut oil

2 medium (300g) onions, chopped

2 tablespoons mild curry powder

1 teaspoon ground turmeric

1 teaspoon ground coriander

1 teaspoon ground cumin

400g can tomatoes

300g cauliflower, chopped

300g broccoli, chopped

1 medium (120g) carrot, sliced

2 medium (240g) zucchini, sliced

1 tablespoon lemon juice

1/2 cup (125ml) vegetable stock

1 tablespoon plain flour

1 tablespoon water

1/2 cup (75g) roasted cashews

Combine oil, onion and spices in large microwave-safe bowl; cook, uncovered, on HIGH (100%) 5 minutes, stirring once during cooking. Add undrained crushed tomatoes and cauliflower; cook, covered, on HIGH (100%) 3 minutes.

Stir in remaining vegetables, juice and stock; cook, covered, on HIGH (100%) 8 minutes, stirring once during cooking. Stir in blended flour and water; cook, covered, on HIGH (100%) about 4 minutes or until vegetables are tender, stirring once during cooking. Stir in nuts.

On the table in 30 minutes

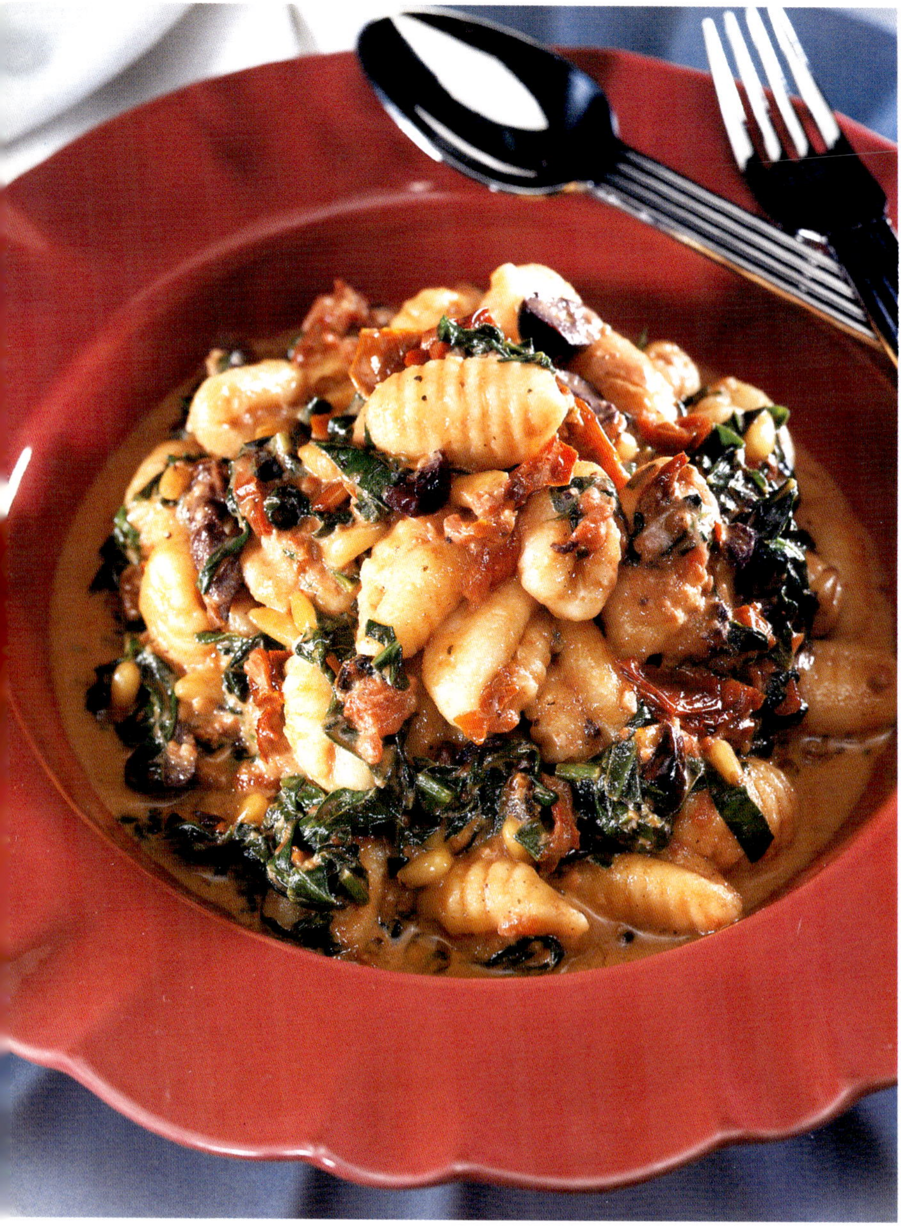

gnocchi with spinach, 25
tomato and pine nuts

1/2 cup (80g) pine nuts
3/4 cup (180ml) cream
400g can tomatoes
3 cloves garlic, crushed
1/2 cup (75g) drained chopped sun-dried tomatoes in oil
1/2 cup (60g) seeded black olives, sliced
750g packaged potato gnocchi
1.5 litres (6 cups) boiling water
500g spinach, chopped coarsely

Place nuts in large shallow microwave-safe dish; cook, uncovered, on HIGH (100%) about 6 minutes or until browned lightly, stirring 3 times during cooking.

Combine cream, undrained crushed canned tomatoes and garlic in large microwave-safe bowl; cook, uncovered, on HIGH (100%) 5 minutes. Add sun-dried tomatoes and olives; cook, uncovered, on HIGH (100%) 2 minutes. Cover to keep warm.

Place gnocchi in large microwave-safe bowl, cover with boiling water; cook, uncovered, on HIGH (100%) 2 minutes. Drain gnocchi, gently toss in large microwave-safe bowl with tomato sauce, nuts and spinach; cook, uncovered, on HIGH (100%) 2 minutes.

On the table in 30 minutes

26 bacon and beef loaf
with plum sauce

cooking oil spray

6 bacon rashers

500g minced beef

1 small (80g) onion, chopped finely

1 small (70g) carrot, grated coarsely

2 eggs, beaten lightly

1 tablespoon tomato paste

130g can creamed corn

1 cup (70g) stale breadcrumbs

1 tablespoon chopped fresh parsley

plum sauce

1/2 cup (125ml) plum sauce

1/2 cup (125ml) beef stock

Coat 12cm x 21cm rectangular microwave-safe dish with cooking oil spray, line base and sides with overlapping bacon rashers.
Using hand, combine beef, onion, carrot, eggs, paste, corn, breadcrumbs and parsley in large bowl; press firmly over bacon in dish. Fold ends of bacon over meatloaf. Cook, uncovered, on HIGH (100%) 20 minutes; drain away excess fat halfway through cooking. Stand, covered, 5 minutes before serving with Plum Sauce.
Plum Sauce Combine both ingredients in microwave-safe jug. Cook, uncovered, on HIGH (100%) 1 minute.

On the table in 45 minutes

sang choy bow

20 (500g) medium uncooked prawns

1 teaspoon sesame oil

1 medium (150g) onion, chopped finely

3 cloves garlic, crushed

1 tablespoon grated fresh ginger

1 medium (120g) carrot, chopped finely

2 sticks celery, chopped finely

750g minced beef

2 teaspoons sambal oelek

2 teaspoons black bean sauce

1 tablespoon soy sauce

2 tablespoons oyster sauce

2 teaspoons cornflour

2 tablespoons chopped fresh coriander leaves

8 lettuce leaves

On the table in 40 minutes

Shell and devein prawns; process prawns until almost smooth.

Combine oil, onion, garlic, ginger, carrot and celery in large microwave-safe bowl; cook, uncovered, on HIGH (100%) 2 minutes, stirring once during cooking. Stir in beef and sambal oelek; cook, uncovered, on HIGH (100%) 8 minutes, stirring once during cooking.

Stir in prawns, cook, uncovered, on HIGH (100%) 5 minutes. Stir in blended sauces and cornflour; cook, uncovered, on HIGH (100%) about 5 minutes or until mixture boils and thickens slightly, stirring twice during cooking.

Stir in coriander; serve in lettuce leaves.

28 camembert pastrami chicken

4 (680g) chicken breast fillets
125g camembert cheese, sliced
50g shaved pastrami

Cut a slit along the thickest side of each chicken breast to form a pocket. Fill each pocket with slices of cheese and shavings of pastrami; secure opening with toothpicks.

Place chicken, in single layer, in large shallow microwave-safe dish; cook, covered, on HIGH (100%) about 8 minutes or until chicken is cooked through. Serve with Tomato Basil Sauce.

Tomato Basil Sauce Combine butter, onion and garlic in large microwave-safe bowl; cook, uncovered, on HIGH (100%) 4 minutes, stirring once during cooking. Add undrained crushed tomatoes, paste, water, wine, crumbled stock cube and sauce; cook, covered, on HIGH (100%) 10 minutes. Stir in basil.

tomato basil sauce

30g butter
1 medium (150g) onion, chopped
1 clove garlic, crushed
400g can tomatoes
1 tablespoon tomato paste
1/4 cup (60ml) water
1/4 cup (60ml) dry white wine
1 small chicken stock cube
1 teaspoon Worcestershire sauce
1 tablespoon chopped fresh basil leaves

On the table in 35 minutes

chicken, tomato and leek casserole

29

30g butter

1 medium (350g) leek, sliced

1 clove garlic, crushed

300g can Tomato Supreme

2 medium (240g) zucchini, sliced

¼ cup (60ml) dry white wine

6 (660g) chicken thigh fillets, chopped

200g button mushrooms, sliced

1 tablespoon chopped fresh basil leaves

1 tablespoon chopped fresh parsley

Combine butter, leek and garlic in large microwave-safe bowl; cook, uncovered, on HIGH (100%) 4 minutes, stirring once during cooking. Add Tomato Supreme, zucchini and wine; cook, covered, on HIGH (100%) 5 minutes. Add chicken, mushrooms and herbs; cook, covered, on HIGH (100%) about 12 minutes or until chicken is cooked through, stirring twice during cooking.

On the table in 30 minutes

30 fish cutlets in herb tomato sauce

425g can tomato puree

1 medium (150g) onion, chopped finely

1 tablespoon chopped fresh parsley

1 tablespoon chopped fresh oregano

2 teaspoons chopped fresh thyme

1 clove garlic, crushed

2 small chicken stock cubes

1 teaspoon sugar

4 (1kg) white fish cutlets

Combine puree, onion, herbs, garlic, crumbled stock cubes and sugar in large microwave-safe bowl; cook, covered, on HIGH (100%) 5 minutes, stirring once during cooking.
Place fish, in single layer, in large shallow microwave-safe dish; cook, covered, on HIGH (100%) 4 minutes. Pour tomato mixture over fish; cook, covered, on HIGH (100%) about 5 minutes or until fish is cooked through.

On the table in 25 minutes

cheese and herb stuffed potatoes

31

4 large (1.2kg) potatoes

2 teaspoons olive oil

$1/2$ teaspoon seasoned pepper

30g butter

60g packaged cream cheese, chopped

1 tablespoon milk

1 tablespoon chopped fresh parsley

1 tablespoon olive oil, extra

1 clove garlic, crushed

2 bacon rashers, chopped

2 green onions, chopped

2 tablespoons finely grated parmesan cheese

Prick potatoes all over with fork, rub with combined oil and pepper. Place potatoes around edge of large shallow microwave-safe dish; cook, uncovered, on HIGH (100%) about 15 minutes or until potatoes are just tender. Stand potatoes 5 minutes.

Cut tops from potatoes, scoop out flesh, leaving 1.5cm thick shells. Mash potato flesh with butter, cream cheese, milk and parsley in medium bowl.

Meanwhile, combine extra oil, garlic and bacon in small microwave-safe bowl; cook, uncovered, on HIGH (100%) 3 minutes. Add onion and parmesan cheese; mix well.

Combine half the bacon mixture with potato mixture in bowl, spoon into potato shells; sprinkle with remaining bacon mixture. Place filled potatoes in large shallow microwave-safe dish; cook, uncovered, on HIGH (100%) 3 minutes.

On the table in 25 minutes

32 vegetables in the microwave

The microwave oven stars when it comes to cooking vegetables. It cooks them very quickly which means they retain their nutrients, their flavour and their colour. If you don't want to cover the dish with plastic wrap, use a snug-fitting plate or saucer. All vegetables should be cooked on HIGH and drained immediately after cooking.

Asparagus (250g)
Snap off woody ends and, if the spears are thick, peel them with a vegetable peeler. Place in dish with 2 tablespoons water, cover with plastic wrap and cook about 2 minutes.

Broccoli and Cauliflower (250g)
Cut into florets, cut thick stems into slices. Place in dish (stem end towards edge) with 2 tablespoons water, cover with plastic wrap and cook about 3 minutes, depending on size of florets. Allow about 10 minutes to cook a whole cauliflower in the microwave.

Brussels sprouts (250g)
Remove tough-looking outer leaves and cut a thin slice off base. Score a cross in base of each sprout, place in dish with 2 tablespoons water, cover with plastic wrap and cook about 3 minutes, depending on size of sprouts.

Cabbage (half a cabbage)
Shred cabbage, place in a strainer and rinse with cold water. Place in dish with a knob of butter (if desired) but no extra water, cover with plastic wrap and cook about 4 minutes or until tender.

Carrots (250g)
Cut into slices or sticks, place in dish with 2 tablespoons water, cover with plastic wrap and cook about 3 minutes.

Corn (2 cobs)
Remove husks and silk. Wrap each cob in plastic wrap, place on microwave turntable and cook about 5 minutes.

Green beans (250g)
Top and tail beans. Place in dish with 2 tablespoons water, cover with plastic wrap and cook about 3 minutes for whole beans, 2-3 minutes for sliced beans.

Mushrooms (250g)
Slice, place in dish with about a tablespoon of butter, cover with plastic wrap and cook 1 minute. Lift plastic and stir to distribute melted butter, cover again and cook about 1 minute.

Peas (250g shelled)
Place in dish with 2 tablespoons water, cover with plastic wrap and cook about 3 minutes.
To cook frozen peas, place in dish with no water, cover with plastic wrap and cook about 2 minutes.

Potatoes (250g)
Cut into quarters (peeled or unpeeled), place in dish with 2 tablespoons water, cover with plastic wrap and cook about 4 minutes.
To cook a whole potato, rub with oil if desired, pierce the skin in several places with a fork and cook about 5 minutes.

Pumpkin (250g)
Peel and cut into chunks. Place in dish with 2 tablespoons water, cover with plastic wrap and cook about 4 minutes.

Silverbeet and Spinach (500g)
Trim and shred leaves, rinse with cold water. Place in dish with no additional water, cover with plastic wrap and cook about 3 minutes.

34 savoury mince with fresh herbs

1 tablespoon olive oil

2 medium (300g) onions, chopped

1 large (180g) carrot, chopped

3 cloves garlic, crushed

1kg minced beef

4 medium (480g) zucchini, chopped

400g can tomatoes

2/3 cup (160ml) tomato paste

2 tablespoons Worcestershire sauce

2 beef stock cubes

2 tablespoons fruit chutney

1/4 cup chopped fresh oregano leaves

2 tablespoons chopped fresh basil leaves

1 tablespoon chopped fresh parsley

1 cup (125g) frozen peas, thawed

Combine oil, onion, carrot and garlic in large microwave-safe bowl; cook, covered, on HIGH (100%) 10 minutes, stirring once during cooking. Stir in beef; cook, covered, on HIGH (100%) 7 minutes, stirring once during cooking. **Add** zucchini, undrained crushed tomatoes, paste, sauce, crumbled stock cubes, chutney and herbs; cook, covered, on HIGH (100%) 15 minutes, stirring 3 times during cooking. Stir in peas; cook, covered, on HIGH (100%) 5 minutes.

On the table in 45 minutes

individual cheese and spinach meatloaves

35

150g spinach, chopped coarsely

2 tablespoons water

40g cheddar cheese

2 tablespoons barbecue sauce

750g minced beef

1/2 cup (35g) stale breadcrumbs

3 green onions, chopped

1 tablespoon tomato paste

1 teaspoon seasoned pepper

1/2 teaspoon garlic powder

Place spinach and water in medium microwave-safe bowl; cook, covered, on HIGH (100%) 2 minutes, drain. Squeeze excess liquid from spinach; shred finely. Cut cheese into 4 cubes.

Brush four 1-cup (250ml) microwave-safe dishes with half the barbecue sauce.

Using hand, combine beef, breadcrumbs, onion, paste, pepper and powder in large bowl; shape into 4 patties. Make a hollow in the centre of each patty, push one-quarter of the spinach and a cube of cheese into centre of each patty, shape into round patties to enclose filling completely. Press into prepared dishes. Spread remaining barbecue sauce over top of patties.

Cook, uncovered, on MEDIUM-HIGH (70%) about 12 minutes or until firm. Stand, covered, 5 minutes, drain away liquid; turn out patties.

On the table in 35 minutes

36 noodles
primavera

1 tablespoon olive oil

1 medium (150g) onion, sliced

1 clove garlic, crushed

500g asparagus, trimmed, cut into pieces

2 cups (250g) frozen peas

300ml cream

$1/4$ cup (60ml) vegetable stock

2 tablespoons Dijon mustard

$1/3$ cup (25g) coarsely grated parmesan cheese

$1/4$ cup chopped fresh mint leaves

375g thick fresh egg noodles

4 cups (1 litre) boiling water

Combine oil, onion and garlic in large microwave-safe bowl; cook, uncovered, on HIGH (100%) 4 minutes, stirring once during cooking. Add asparagus, peas, cream, stock and mustard; cook, uncovered, on HIGH (100%) 10 minutes, stirring twice during cooking. Stir in cheese and mint.
Place noodles in large microwave-safe bowl, cover with boiling water; cook, uncovered, on HIGH (100%) 3 minutes. Drain noodles. Gently toss noodles in large bowl with asparagus and cream mixture.

On the table in 25 minutes

cheesy lamb fillets 37
with quick tomato sauce

8 (640g) lamb fillets

3/4 cup (150g) ricotta cheese

2 tablespoons finely grated parmesan cheese

1 tablespoon Worcestershire sauce

quick tomato sauce

300g can Tomato Supreme

1 tablespoon tomato paste

1 tablespoon chopped fresh parsley

2 teaspoons chopped fresh oregano

Remove fat and sinew from lamb; flatten with mallet until 2mm thick. Spread lamb with combined cheeses, fold fillets in half to enclose filling; secure with toothpicks.

Place lamb in large shallow microwave-safe dish; brush with Worcestershire sauce. Cook, uncovered, on HIGH (100%) about 5 minutes or until lamb is cooked as desired. Remove toothpicks; serve with Quick Tomato Sauce.

Quick Tomato Sauce Combine all ingredients in small microwave-safe bowl; cook, uncovered, on HIGH (100%) 2 minutes.

On the table in 20 minutes

38 devilled chicken

20g butter

¼ cup (60ml) tomato sauce

1 tablespoon soy sauce

2 teaspoons Worcestershire sauce

2 tablespoons fruit chutney

2 tablespoons brown sugar

1 teaspoon mild curry powder

8 (1kg) chicken lovely legs

Place butter in large shallow microwave-safe dish; cook, uncovered, on HIGH (100%) 30 seconds. Add remaining ingredients, coating chicken with curry mixture.

Arrange chicken around edge of dish; cook, uncovered, on HIGH (100%) 15 minutes or until chicken is cooked through, brushing with sauce mixture twice during cooking. Serve hot or cold.

On the table in 25 minutes

fish rolls 39
with creamy dill mayonnaise

We used whiting fillets in this recipe.

8 small (800g) white fish fillets

1/3 cup (35g) packaged breadcrumbs

2 tablespoons chopped fresh parsley

1 tablespoon lemon juice

8 (400g) large uncooked prawns, shelled

1/4 cup (60ml) dry white wine

1/4 cup (60ml) lemon juice, extra

30g butter, chopped

creamy dill mayonnaise

2/3 cup (160ml) mayonnaise

1/3 cup (80ml) thickened cream

2 teaspoons lemon juice

1 teaspoon chopped fresh dill

Top each fish fillet with combined breadcrumbs, parsley and juice; top with prawns. Roll fish up to enclose prawns, secure with toothpicks.
Place fish rolls, in single layer, in large shallow microwave-safe dish; pour over combined wine and extra juice, top with butter. Cook, covered, on HIGH (100%) about 7 minutes or until seafood is cooked through.
Remove toothpicks; serve with Creamy Dill Mayonnaise.
Creamy Dill Mayonnaise Combine all ingredients in small bowl.
On the table in 20 minutes

40 bolognese sauce

1 tablespoon olive oil

1 large (200g) onion, chopped

3 cloves garlic, crushed

3 bacon rashers, chopped

200g button mushrooms, sliced

1kg minced beef

400g can tomatoes

3/4 cup (180ml) tomato paste

1/2 cup (125ml) dry red wine

1 beef stock cube

Combine oil, onion, garlic and bacon in large microwave-safe bowl; cook, covered, on HIGH (100%) 6 minutes, stirring once during cooking. Stir in mushrooms; cook, uncovered, on HIGH (100%) 4 minutes. Add beef, stir well; cook, covered, on HIGH (100%) 10 minutes, stirring twice during cooking.

Add undrained crushed tomatoes, paste, wine and crumbled stock cube; cook, uncovered, on HIGH (100%) about 20 minutes or until sauce thickens, stirring twice during cooking.

On the table in 45 minutes

crab and sweet corn 41
soup

2 teaspoons sesame oil

4 green onions, sliced thinly

4 cups (1 litre) chicken stock

2 x 310g cans creamed corn

1 tablespoon salt-reduced soy sauce

1 tablespoon cornflour

1 tablespoon water

250g cooked or canned crab meat

Combine oil and onion in large microwave-safe bowl; cook, uncovered, on HIGH (100%) 1 minute. Add stock, corn, sauce and blended cornflour and water; cook, uncovered, on HIGH (100%) about 10 minutes or until soup boils and thickens slightly, stirring twice during cooking. Stir in shredded crab meat; cook, uncovered, on HIGH (100%) 2 minutes.

On the table in 20 minutes

42 mince and macaroni casserole

250g macaroni pasta
1.5 litres (6 cups) boiling water
30g butter
2 medium (300g) onions, chopped finely
3 cloves garlic, crushed
500g minced beef
1/3 cup (50g) plain flour
2 tablespoons tomato paste
1 teaspoon mild English mustard
3 cups (750ml) milk
1 cup (125g) coarsely grated cheddar cheese
1 cup (100g) coarsely grated mozzarella cheese
1/4 cup chopped fresh flat-leaf parsley

Spread pasta over base of 3-litre (12-cup) deep microwave-safe dish, cover with the boiling water; cook, uncovered, on HIGH (100%) about 10 minutes or until just tender, stirring twice during cooking. Drain pasta, cover to keep warm while preparing the sauce.

Combine butter, onion and garlic in same dish; cook, uncovered, on HIGH (100%) 5 minutes. Stir in beef; cook, uncovered, on HIGH (100%) 10 minutes, stirring twice during cooking. Stir in flour, paste and mustard; cook, uncovered, on HIGH (100%) 2 minutes. Stir in milk; cook, uncovered, on HIGH (100%) about 6 minutes or until mixture boils and thickens, stirring twice during cooking.

Stir in pasta and half the combined cheeses and parsley. Top with remaining cheese and parsley mixture; cook, uncovered, on HIGH (100%) about 2 minutes or until cheese melts.

On the table in 45 minutes

44 marinated sesame
drumsticks

8 (1.2kg) chicken drumsticks
¼ cup (60ml) soy sauce
2 tablespoons hoi sin sauce
1 tablespoon sweet sherry
1 tablespoon honey
1 tablespoon sesame seeds
2 cloves garlic, crushed
2 teaspoons grated fresh ginger

On the table in 30 minutes

Place chicken in large shallow microwave-safe dish; pour over combined remaining ingredients. Cover; stand 10 minutes.

Arrange chicken, in single layer, in same dish, with thick ends towards edge of dish; brush with marinade. Cover with absorbent paper; cook on HIGH (100%) about 15 minutes or until chicken is cooked through, brushing with marinade twice during cooking.

creamy bacon and basil
tagliatelle

45

500g tagliatelle pasta

2 litres (8 cups) boiling water

4 bacon rashers, sliced thinly

300ml cream

1/3 cup (80ml) dry white wine

2 teaspoons seeded mustard

2 tablespoons finely grated parmesan cheese

1 tablespoon cornflour

2 tablespoons water

1/2 cup chopped fresh basil leaves

6 green onions, chopped

Place pasta in large microwave-safe bowl, cover with boiling water; cook, uncovered, on HIGH (100%) about 12 minutes or until just tender, stirring twice during cooking. Drain pasta, cover to keep warm.
Place bacon between 4 sheets of absorbent paper; cook on HIGH (100%) about 3 minutes or until bacon is crisp.
Combine bacon, cream, wine, mustard, cheese and blended cornflour and water in large microwave-safe bowl; cook, uncovered, on HIGH (100%) 4 minutes or until sauce boils and thickens, stirring once during cooking. Stir in basil and onion. Serve pasta with creamy bacon sauce.
On the table in 30 minutes

46 chilli meatballs
in tomato sauce

500g minced beef

8 green onions, chopped

1 clove garlic, crushed

1 tablespoon tomato paste

1/2 cup (35g) stale breadcrumbs

2 tablespoons chopped fresh parsley

1 egg

plain flour

400g can tomatoes

1/2 teaspoon chilli powder

1 teaspoon Worcestershire sauce

2 tablespoons dry white wine

Using hand, combine beef, half the onion, garlic, paste, breadcrumbs, parsley and egg in large bowl; shape into 8 meatballs. Toss in flour; shake off excess. Place meatballs around edge of large shallow microwave-safe dish.

Combine undrained crushed tomatoes and remaining ingredients in bowl; pour over meatballs in dish. Cook, covered, on MEDIUM (55%) 20 minutes. Uncover; cook on MEDIUM (55%) 10 minutes.

On the table in 40 minutes

risotto
napoletana

2 tablespoons olive oil

1 large (200g) onion, chopped

1½ cups (300g) arborio rice

400g can tomatoes

3 cups (750ml) boiling water

100g thin slices spicy salami, chopped coarsely

¼ cup (35g) sliced sun-dried tomatoes in oil, drained

½ cup (60g) seeded black olives, sliced

½ cup (40g) coarsely grated parmesan cheese

Combine oil and onion in large microwave-safe bowl; cook, uncovered, on HIGH (100%) 5 minutes, stirring once during cooking. Stir in rice; cook, uncovered, on HIGH (100%) 1 minute. Add undrained crushed tomatoes and the boiling water; cook, covered, on HIGH (100%) 10 minutes, stirring twice during cooking. Stand, covered, 5 minutes. Stir in remaining ingredients.

On the table in 30 minutes

48 spinach and pumpkin
curry

1 tablespoon flaked almonds
1kg butternut pumpkin
2 tablespoons ghee
2 medium (300g) onions, sliced
2 cloves garlic, crushed
1 teaspoon grated fresh ginger
2 small fresh green chillies, sliced thinly
1 teaspoon ground coriander
1 teaspoon ground cumin
1 teaspoon black mustard seeds
1/2 teaspoon ground turmeric
300ml cream
250g spinach, chopped coarsely
2 tablespoons chopped fresh coriander leaves

Place nuts in small shallow microwave-safe dish; cook, uncovered, on HIGH (100%) about 4 minutes or until nuts are browned lightly, stirring twice during cooking. Peel pumpkin, cut into 3cm pieces.

Combine ghee and onion in large microwave-safe bowl; cook, uncovered, on HIGH (100%) about 10 minutes or until browned lightly, stirring 3 times during cooking. Add garlic, ginger, chilli and spices; cook, uncovered, on HIGH (100%) 30 seconds. Add pumpkin and cream; cook, covered, on HIGH (100%) about 12 minutes or until pumpkin is just tender, stirring gently twice during cooking. Add spinach and coriander; cook, uncovered, on HIGH (100%) 1 minute. Just before serving, sprinkle with nuts.

On the table in 35 minutes

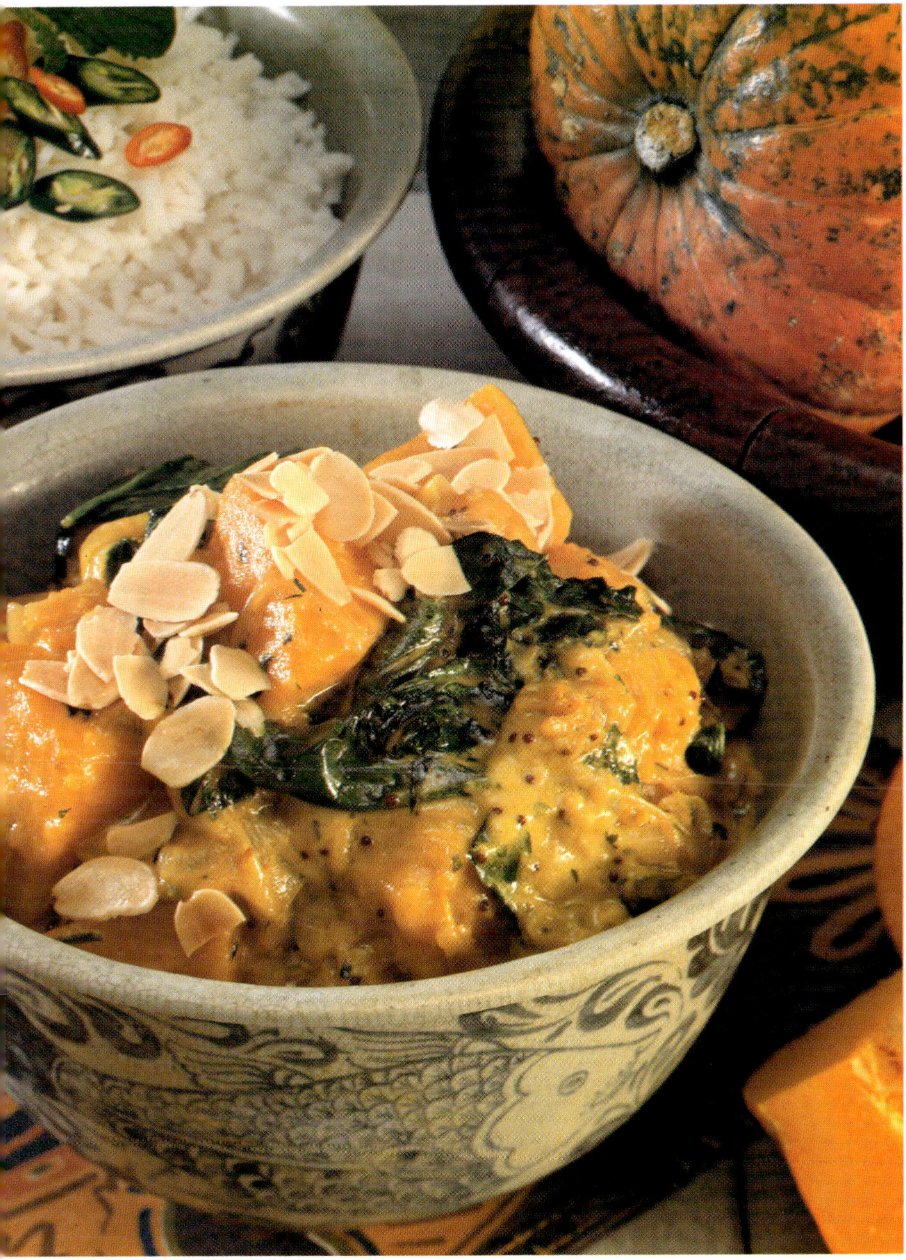

50 chicken burritos

Combine chicken, salsa and water in large microwave-safe bowl; cook, covered, on HIGH (100%) 5 minutes, stirring once during cooking. **Heat** tortillas in microwave, according to directions on the packet. **Divide** chicken mixture among tortillas; top with lettuce, cheese and tomato. Roll up into cigar shapes.

You will need 1 cooked chicken for this recipe.

2 1/2 cups (425g) finely chopped cooked chicken
3 cups (750ml) bottled salsa
1/3 cup (80ml) water
8 x 20cm flour tortillas
1 cup (100g) shredded lettuce
1 cup (125g) grated cheddar cheese
1 large (250g) tomato, chopped finely

On the table in 20 minutes

peppered chicken 51
with creamy sauce

20g butter

1 clove garlic, crushed

4 (680g) chicken breast fillets

coarsely ground black pepper

creamy sauce

30g butter

2 tablespoons plain flour

1 chicken stock cube

3/4 cup (180ml) cream

1/4 cup (60ml) dry white wine

1 tablespoon marsala

Combine butter and garlic in small microwave-safe bowl; cook, uncovered, on HIGH (100%) 30 seconds. Brush chicken with butter; then sprinkle both sides with pepper.

Place chicken, in single layer, in large shallow microwave-safe dish. Cook, covered, on HIGH (100%) 3 minutes. Pour Creamy Sauce over chicken in dish; cook, covered, on HIGH (100%) about 6 minutes or until chicken is cooked through and sauce has thickened, whisking sauce twice during cooking.

Creamy Sauce Combine butter in small microwave-safe bowl; cook, uncovered, on HIGH (100%) 30 seconds. Whisk in remaining ingredients.

On the table in 20 minutes

52 apricot lamb with honey sauce

Ask your butcher to butterfly a 1.5kg leg of lamb for you.

¼ cup (40g) burghul

⅓ cup (50g) chopped dried apricots

2 green onions, chopped

2 tablespoons pine nuts

1½ tablespoons fruit chutney

1kg butterflied leg of lamb

Place burghul in small heatproof bowl, cover with boiling water; stand 10 minutes. Drain, rinse and pat dry with absorbent paper. Combine burghul, apricots, onion, nuts and chutney in bowl.

Open lamb out flat, fat-side down, spread with apricot mixture, roll up from short side; secure with string at 2cm intervals. Place lamb, seam side down, on microwave-safe roasting rack; cook, uncovered, on HIGH (100%) 10 minutes. Turn lamb; cook, uncovered, on MEDIUM-HIGH (70%) 20 minutes, turning once. Cover lamb; stand 5 minutes. Serve with Honey Sauce.

Honey Sauce Combine all ingredients in small microwave-safe bowl; cook, uncovered, on HIGH (100%) about 3 minutes or until sauce boils and thickens, whisking once.

honey sauce

⅓ cup (80ml) honey

⅓ cup (80ml) orange juice

1½ tablespoons soy sauce

2 teaspoons grated fresh ginger

2 teaspoons cornflour blended with 2 tablespoons water

On the table in 40 minutes

spaghetti 53
with prawns, coriander and peanuts

250g spaghetti

1.5 litres (6 cups) boiling water

40 (1kg) medium uncooked prawns

¼ cup (60ml) peanut oil

1 large (350g) red capsicum, sliced thinly

⅓ cup (50g) chopped peanuts

⅓ cup (80ml) lime juice

2 tablespoons sweet chilli sauce

½ cup chopped fresh coriander leaves

Break pasta in half, place in large microwave-safe bowl, cover with the boiling water; cook, uncovered, on HIGH (100%) about 12 minutes or until just tender, stirring twice during cooking. Drain. **Shell** and devein prawns, leaving tails intact. Combine half the oil, prawns, capsicum and nuts in large microwave-safe bowl; cook, uncovered, on HIGH (100%) about 5 minutes or until prawns change in colour, stirring once during cooking. Add pasta, remaining oil, juice and sauce; cook, uncovered, on HIGH (100%) 4 minutes, stirring once during cooking. Mix in chopped coriander

On the table in 40 minutes

54 beef and vegetable curry

1 medium (150g) onion, chopped

2/3 cup (160ml) mild curry paste

1kg minced beef

400g can tomatoes

1 large (500g) kumara, chopped

1 medium (300g) eggplant, chopped

1 cup (250ml) beef stock

1 cup (125g) frozen peas

1/4 cup chopped fresh coriander leaves

On the table in 45 minutes

Combine onion and paste in large microwave-safe bowl; cook, covered, on HIGH (100%) 5 minutes, stirring once during cooking. Add beef; cook, covered, on HIGH (100%) 10 minutes, stirring twice during cooking. Add undrained crushed tomatoes, kumara, eggplant and stock; cook, uncovered, on HIGH (100%) 20 minutes, stirring twice during cooking. Add peas; cook, uncovered, on HIGH (100%) 5 minutes. Stir in coriander.

seafood curry

2 medium (400g) squid hoods

30 (750g) medium uncooked prawns

500g firm white fish fillets

1 tablespoon olive oil

1 large (200g) onion, sliced

2 large (600g) potatoes, chopped

1/3 cup (80ml) mild curry paste

1 1/2 cups (375ml) chicken stock

1 cup (250ml) coconut cream

300g scallops

200g sugar snap peas

1 tablespoon chopped fresh coriander leaves

Cut squid hoods open, cut shallow diagonal slashes in criss-cross pattern on inside surface; cut into 1 x 6cm pieces. Shell and devein prawns, leaving tails intact. Cut fish into 4cm pieces.

Combine oil, onion and potato in large microwave-safe bowl; cook, uncovered, on HIGH (100%) 3 minutes. Add paste; cook, uncovered, on HIGH (100%) 2 minutes. Stir in stock; cook, uncovered, on HIGH (100%) 5 minutes. Add coconut cream and seafood; cook, uncovered, on HIGH (100%) about 12 minutes or until seafood is cooked through, stirring gently twice during cooking. Add peas; cook, uncovered, on HIGH (100%) 1 minute. Serve sprinkled with coriander.

On the table in 45 minutes

56 roman tomato soup

2 bacon rashers, chopped finely

1 tablespoon olive oil

2 cloves garlic, crushed

1 medium (150g) onion, chopped finely

420g can condensed tomato soup

400g can tomatoes

3 cups (750ml) boiling water

2 cups (210g) small fusilli (spiral pasta)

1 tablespoon finely chopped fresh basil leaves

On the table in 35 minutes

Place bacon between 4 sheets of absorbent paper; cook on HIGH (100%) about 2 minutes or until bacon is crisp.
Combine oil, garlic and onion in large microwave-safe bowl; cook, uncovered, on HIGH (100%) 4 minutes, stirring once during cooking. Add undiluted soup, undrained crushed tomatoes, the boiling water and pasta; cook, uncovered, on HIGH (100%) about 15 minutes or until pasta is just tender, stirring twice during cooking. Stir in basil. Ladle soup into bowls; sprinkle with bacon.

…

italian fish fillets

57

30g butter

1 medium (150g) onion, chopped

1 clove garlic, crushed

400g can tomatoes

1 teaspoon sugar

2 tablespoons fresh oregano leaves

4 medium (800g) white fish fillets

Combine butter, onion and garlic in large microwave-safe bowl; cook, covered, on HIGH (100%) 4 minutes, stirring once during cooking.
Add undrained crushed tomatoes to onion mixture in bowl, stir in sugar and oregano. Cook a further 2 minutes on HIGH (100%).
Place fish, in single layer, in large shallow microwave-safe dish. Cook, covered, on HIGH (100%) 1 minute, turn fish and cook 2 minutes on HIGH (100%) or until cooked through. Spoon sauce over fish.

On the table in 15 minutes

58 seafood marinara

400g spaghetti

2 litres (8 cups) boiling water

1 tablespoon olive oil

1 medium (150g) onion, chopped

1 clove garlic, crushed

400g can tomatoes

1/4 cup (60ml) dry white wine

1/4 cup (60ml) water

2 tablespoons tomato paste

2 tablespoons cornflour

2 tablespoons water, extra

5 (250g) large uncooked prawns, shelled, halved

2 (400g) white fish fillets, chopped

250g scallops

1 tablespoon chopped fresh parsley

1 tablespoon chopped fresh basil leaves

Break pasta in half, place in large microwave-safe bowl, cover with the boiling water; cook, uncovered, on HIGH (100%) about 12 minutes or until just tender, stirring twice during cooking. Drain pasta, cover to keep warm.

Combine oil, onion and garlic in large microwave-safe bowl; cook, uncovered, on HIGH (100%) 4 minutes, stirring once during cooking. Add undrained crushed tomatoes, wine, water and paste; cook, covered, on HIGH (100%) 10 minutes. Stir in blended cornflour and extra water; cook, uncovered, on HIGH (100%) 1 minute or until sauce boils and thickens.

Place seafood in large shallow microwave-safe dish; cook, covered, on HIGH (100%) 4 minutes or until just tender, stirring once during cooking. Stir undrained seafood and herbs into hot tomato sauce; serve with pasta.

On the table in 40 minutes

glossary

bacon rasher also known as slices of bacon.
barbecue sauce a spicy, tomato-based sauce used to marinate and baste, or as an accompaniment.
bean sprouts also known as bean shoots.
beef
corned silverside: cut from the outside of the upper leg and cured.
mince: also known as ground beef.
black bean sauce a Chinese sauce made from fermented soy beans.
breadcrumbs
packaged: fine-textured, crunchy, purchased white breadcrumbs.
stale: one- or two-day-old bread made into crumbs by grating, blending or processing.
burghul wheat that is steamed until partly cooked, cracked then dried.
butter 125g is equal to 1 stick butter.
capsicum also known as bell pepper.
chicken
lovely leg: also known as drummette. Skinless drumstick with the end of the bone removed.
tenderloin: the thin strip of meat lying under the breast.
chilli
powder: the Asian variety is the hottest, made from ground chillies; it can be used as a substitute for fresh chillies in the proportion of $1/2$ teaspoon ground chilli powder to 1 medium fresh chilli.
jalapeno pepper: fairly hot green chillies, available in brine bottled or fresh from specialty greengrocers.
coconut
cream: available in cans and cartons; made from coconut and water.
milk: pure, unsweetened coconut milk available in cans.
cornflour also known as cornstarch.
curry leaves shiny bright-green, sharp-ended leaves, used fresh or dried.
eggplant also known as aubergine.
fish
Atlantic salmon: now farmed widely. Available whole, or as steaks, cutlets or fillets.
blue-eye: also known as deep sea trevalla or trevally and blue eye cod; thick, moist white-fleshed fish.
cutlet: crossways slice of fish with bones.
fillets: fish pieces that have been boned and skinned.
flour, plain: an all-purpose flour, made from wheat.
garam masala a powered blend of spices, based on varying proportions of cardamom, cinnamon, cloves, coriander and cumin. Sometimes chilli powder is added.
ghee clarified butter; with milk solids removed, this fat can be heated to a high temperature without burning. Used in Indian cooking.
ginger, fresh also known as green or root ginger; the thick gnarled root of a tropical plant.
herbs 1 teaspoon dried (not ground) is equal to 4 teaspoons chopped fresh herbs.
hoisin sauce a thick, sweet and spicy Chinese paste made from salted fermented soy beans, onions and garlic.
kumara Polynesian name of an orange-fleshed sweet potato often incorrectly called a yam.
lamb
butterflied leg: ask your butcher to butterfly a leg for you, or do it yourself, by cutting along the line of the bone, remove bone and flatten lamb open.
fillets: tenderloin; the smaller piece of meat from a row of loin chops or cutlets.
marsala a sweet fortified wine originally from Sicily.
mushroom
button: small, cultivated white mushrooms having a delicate, subtle flavour.
Chinese dried: also known as shiitake mushrooms; have a meaty flavour.
noodles
2 minute: quick-cook noodles with flavour sachet.

fresh egg: made from wheat flour and eggs; strands vary in thickness.

oil

cooking-oil spray: vegetable oil in an aerosol can, available in supermarkets.

olive: a mono-unsaturated oil, made from the pressing of tree-ripened olives; especially good for everyday cooking and in salad dressings. Light describes the mild flavour, not the fat levels.

peanut: pressed from ground peanuts; most commonly used oil in Asian cooking because of its high smoke point.

sesame: made from roasted, crushed white sesame seeds; a flavouring rather than a cooking medium.

vegetable: any of a number of oils sourced from plants rather than animal fats.

onion, green also known as scallion or (incorrectly) shallot; an immature onion picked before the bulb has formed, having a long, bright-green edible stalk.

oyster sauce Asian in origin, rich, brown sauce made from oysters, brine, salt and soy sauce then thickened with starches.

pastrami a highly seasoned cured and smoked beef, ready to eat when purchased.

pine nut also known as pignoli; small, cream coloured kernels obtained from the cones of different varieties of pine trees.

plum sauce a thick, sweet and sour dipping sauce made from plums, vinegar, sugar, chillies and spices.

prawns also known as shrimp.

pumpkin sometimes used interchangeably with the word squash, the pumpkin is a member of the gourd family used in cooking both as one of many ingredients in a dish or eaten on its own. Various types can be substituted for one another.

rice

arborio: small, round grain rice well-suited to absorb a large amount of liquid; especially suitable for risottos.

basmati: a white, fragrant long-grained rice. It should be washed several times before cooking.

sambal oelek (also ulek or olek) Indonesian in origin, a salty paste made from ground chillies, sugar and spices.

satay sauce traditional Indonesian/Malaysian spicy peanut sauce served with grilled meat skewers.

scallops a bivalve mollusc with fluted shell valve; we use scallops having the coral (roe) attached.

snow peas also called mange tout ("eat all").

spinach the green vegetable often called spinach is correctly known as Swiss chard, silverbeet or seakale.

stock 1 cup (250ml) stock is the equivalent of 1 cup (250ml) water plus 1 crumbled stock cube (or 1 teaspoon stock powder).

sugar snap peas small pods with small, formed peas inside; they are eaten whole, cooked or raw.

tomato

paste: a concentrated tomato puree used to flavour soups, stews, sauces and casseroles.

puree: canned pureed tomatoes (not tomato paste). Use fresh, peeled, pureed tomatoes as a substitute.

sauce: also known as ketchup or catsup; a flavoured condiment made from tomatoes, vinegar and spices.

supreme: a canned product consisting of tomatoes, onions, celery, peppers, cheese and seasonings.

tortilla thin, round unleavened bread originating in Mexico; can be made at home or purchased frozen, fresh or vacuum-packed. Two kinds are available, one made from wheat flour and the other from masa harina (maizemeal).

zucchini also known as courgette.

index

asparagus and chicken risotto 6
bacon and beef loaf with plum sauce 26
bean soup, hearty 13
beef
  and bacon loaf with plum sauce 26
  and vegetable curry 54
  rissoles, country-style 7
  corned with parsley sauce 11
  Mexican chilli 22
bolognese sauce 40
burritos, chicken 50
camembert pastrami chicken 28
casserole
  mince and macaroni 42
  cheese and herb stuffed potatoes 31
cheese and spinach meatloaves, individual 35
chicken
  and asparagus risotto 6
  and potato slice 19
  burritos 50
  drumsticks, marinated sesame 44
  in coconut peanut sauce 14
  camembert pastrami 28
  devilled 38
  peppered, with creamy sauce 51
  saucy, in yogurt 10
  sesame mustard 20
  tomato and leek casserole 29
chowder, vegetable 12
corned beef with parsley sauce 11
crab and sweet corn soup 41
curry
  beef and vegetable 54
  seafood 55
  spinach and pumpkin 48
  vegetable and nut 23

curried vegetable soup 8
drumsticks, marinated sesame 44
fish
  cutlets in herb tomato sauce 30
  fillets, Italian 57
  rolls with creamy dill mayonnaise 39
  creamy mushroom 9
  spicy Indian-style 5
gnocchi with spinach, tomato and pine nuts 25
lamb
  fillets, cheesy, with quick tomato sauce 37
  apricot, with honey sauce 52
macaroni and mince casserole 42
meatballs
  chilli, in tomato sauce 46
  middle eastern-style 17
meatloaves, individual cheese and spinach 35
Mexican chilli beef 22
mince
  and macaroni casserole 42
  savoury, with fresh herbs 34
mushroom fish, creamy 9
mustard chicken, sesame 20
noodles primavera 36
pasta
  creamy bacon and basil tagliatelle 45
  seafood marinara 58
  spaghetti with prawns, coriander and peanuts 53
  tagliatelle, creamy bacon and basil 45
peppered steak, spicy 21
pork, barbecued, stir-fry 15
potatoes, cheese and herb stuffed 31
prawns, spaghetti with coriander, peanuts and 53

primavera noodles 36
pumpkin and leek soup 18
risotto
  napoletana 47
  asparagus and chicken 6
rissoles, country-style beef 7
sang choy bow 27
sauce
  bolognese 40
  coconut peanut, chicken in 14
  creamy dill mayonnaise, fish rolls with 39
  herb tomato, fish cutlets in 30
  honey, apricot lamb with 52
  parsley, corned beef with 11
  plum, bacon and beef loaf with 26
  quick tomato, cheesy, lamb fillets with 37
  tomato, chilli meatballs in 46
savoury mince with fresh herbs 34
seafood
  curry 55
  marinara 58
slice, chicken and potato 19
soup
  crab and sweet corn 41
  curried vegetable 8
  hearty bean 13
  pumpkin and leek 18
  Roman tomato 56
spaghetti with prawns, coriander and peanuts 53
spinach and pumpkin curry 48
steak, spicy peppered 21
stir-fry, barbecued pork 15
tagliatelle, creamy bacon and basil 45
tomato soup, Roman 56
vegetable
  and nut curry 23
  chowder 12
  soup, curried 8
yogurt, saucy chicken in 10

facts and figures 63

These conversions are approximate only, but the difference between an exact and the approximate conversion of various liquid and dry measures is minimal and will not affect your cooking results.

Measuring equipment
The difference between one country's measuring cups and another's is, at most, within a 2 or 3 teaspoon variance. (For the record, 1 Australian metric measuring cup holds approximately 250ml.) The most accurate way of measuring dry ingredients is to weigh them. For liquids, use a clear glass or plastic jug having metric markings.

Note: NZ, Canada, USA and UK all use 15ml tablespoons. Australian tablespoons measure 20ml.
All cup and spoon measurements are level.

How to measure
When using graduated measuring cups, shake dry ingredients loosely into the appropriate cup. Do not tap the cup on a bench or tightly pack the ingredients unless directed to do so. Level the top of measuring cups and measuring spoons with a knife. When measuring liquids, place a clear glass or plastic jug having metric markings on a flat surface to check accuracy at eye level.

Dry Measures

metric	imperial
15g	1/2oz
30g	1oz
60g	2oz
90g	3oz
125g	4oz (1/4lb)
155g	5oz
185g	6oz
220g	7oz
250g	8oz (1/2lb)
280g	9oz
315g	10oz
345g	11oz
375g	12oz (3/4lb)
410g	13oz
440g	14oz
470g	15oz
500g	16oz (1lb)
750g	24oz (1 1/2lb)
1kg	32oz (2lb)

We use large eggs having an average weight of 60g.

Liquid Measures

metric	imperial
30ml	1 fluid oz
60ml	2 fluid oz
100ml	3 fluid oz
125ml	4 fluid oz
150ml	5 fluid oz (1/4 pint/1 gill)
190ml	6 fluid oz
250ml (1cup)	8 fluid oz
300ml	10 fluid oz (1/2 pint)
500ml	16 fluid oz
600ml	20 fluid oz (1 pint)
1000ml (1litre)	1 3/4 pints

Helpful Measures

metric	imperial
3mm	1/8in
6mm	1/4in
1cm	1/2in
2cm	3/4in
2.5cm	1in
6cm	2 1/2in
8cm	3in
20cm	8in
23cm	9in
25cm	10in
30cm	12in (1ft)

Oven Temperatures

These oven temperatures are only a guide.
Always check the manufacturer's manual.

	C°(Celsius)	F°(Fahrenheit)	Gas Mark
Very slow	120	250	1
Slow	150	300	2
Moderately slow	160	325	3
Moderate	180–190	350–375	4
Moderately hot	200–210	400–425	5
Hot	220–230	450–475	6
Very hot	240–250	500–525	7

The Australian Women's Weekly cookbooks

Food editor Pamela Clark
Associate food editor Karen Hammial
Assistant food editor Kathy McGarry
Assistant recipe editor Elizabeth Hooper

Home Library Staff
Editor-in-chief Mary Coleman
Marketing manager Nicole Pizanis
Editor Susan Tomnay
Subeditor Bianca Martin
Concept design Jackie Richards
Designer Jackie Richards
Group publisher Paul Dykzeul

Produced by *The Australian Women's Weekly* Home Library, Sydney.
Colour separations by ACP Colour Graphics Pty Ltd, Sydney.
Printing by Diamond Press Limited, Sydney.
Published by ACP Publishing Pty Limited, 54 Park St, Sydney;
GPO Box 4088, Sydney, NSW 1028. Ph: (02) 9282 8618 Fax: (02) 9267 9438.
AWWHomeLib@publishing.acp.com.au

Australia: Distributed by Network Distribution Company,
GPO Box 4088, Sydney, NSW 1028. Ph: (02) 9282 8777 Fax: (02) 9264 3278.

United Kingdom: Distributed by Australian Consolidated Press (UK),
Moulton Park Business Centre, Red House Rd, Moulton Park, Northampton, NN3 6AQ.
Ph: (01604) 497 531 Fax: (01604) 497 533 Acpukltd@aol.com

Canada: Distributed by Whitecap Books Ltd,
351 Lynn Ave, North Vancouver, BC, V7J 2C4, (604) 980 9852.

New Zealand: Distributed by Netlink Distribution Company,
17B Hargreaves St, Level 5, College Hill, Auckland 1, (9) 302 7616.

South Africa: Distributed by PSD Promotions (Pty) Ltd,
PO Box 1175, Isando 1600, SA, (011) 392 6065.

Make It Tonight: Microwave

Includes index.
ISBN 1 86396 123 2.

1.Microwave cookery I. Title: Australian Women's Weekly.
(Series: Australian Women's Weekly make it tonight mini series).
641.5882

ACP Publishing Pty Limited 1999
ACN 053 273 546

This publication is copyright. No part of it may be reproduced or transmitted
in any form without the written permission of the publishers.

Cover: Italian Fish Fillets, page 57.
Photographer Scott Cameron
Aarabia pasta plate from Inne, Woollahra

Back cover: Saucy Chicken in Yogurt, page 10.